WHAT ON EARTH?

TREES

Kevin Warwick
Pau Morgan

chartwell
books

Branching out into poetry

Can you write a poem about the trees that are growing near you?

Rainbow Fall

Maples are red,
ash leaves turn brown,
holly leaves stay green
all year round.

Beech trees can't really
make up their mind,
for purple or green leaves
are easy to find.

Birch trees and hazel
are easy to see,
with bright yellow leaves
when they fall from the tree.

A rainbow of colors
is out in plain view,
in the leaves of the trees,
just waiting for you.

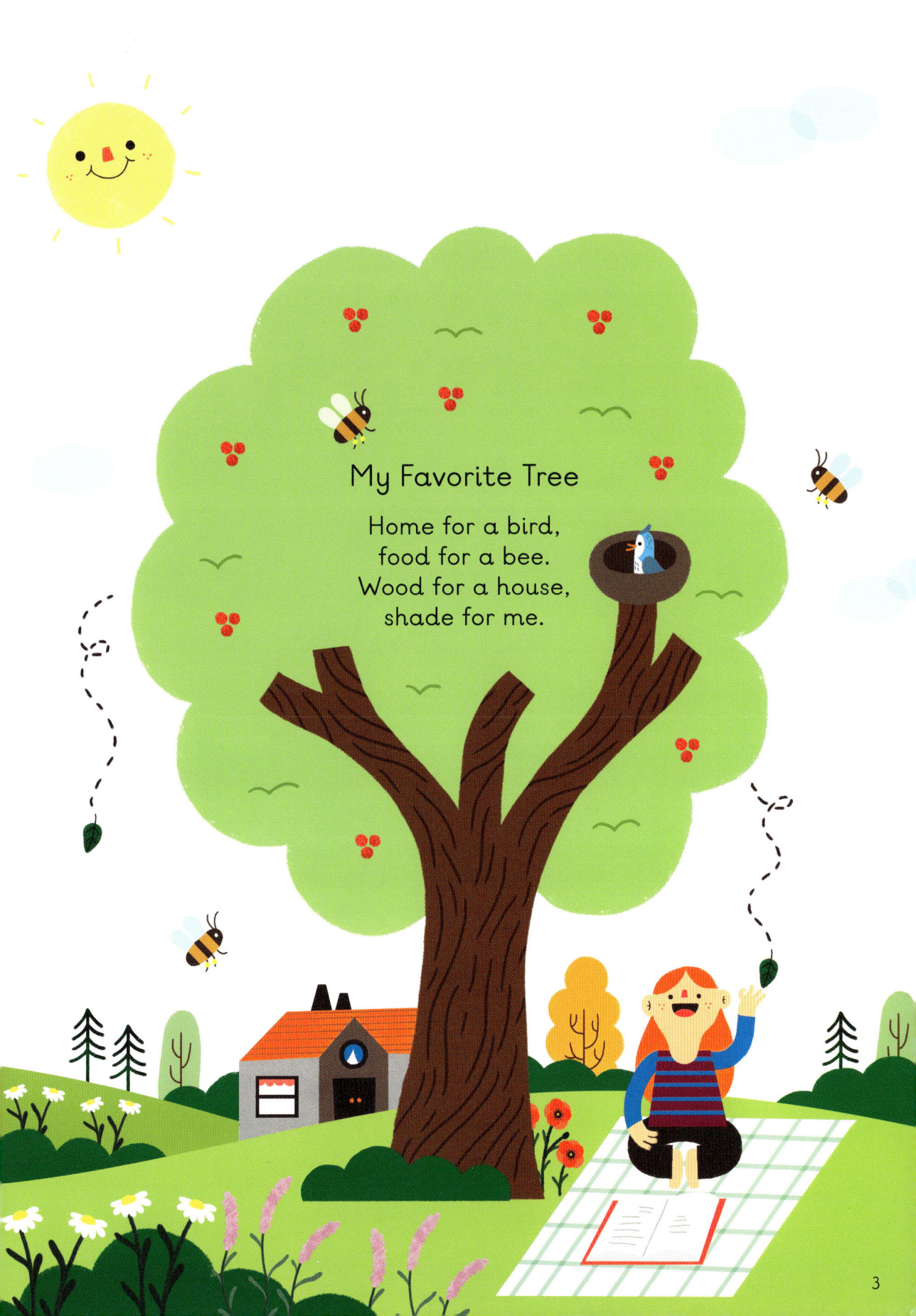

My Favorite Tree

Home for a bird,
food for a bee.
Wood for a house,
shade for me.

What is a tree made of?

Trees come in many different shapes and sizes, but they are all made up of the same parts. Each part has a special job to do.

Fruits grow around tree seeds. The seeds are protected inside the fruit until they are ready to fall from the tree and grow.

If we get the seeds from this apple, we can grow our own trees!

Leaves make food for the tree. Each leaf needs sunshine to do this.

Flowers make the seeds that will grow into new trees.

Bark is the outer layer of the tree. Its job is to protect the inside of the tree.

This woodpecker has a hard time pecking through the tough bark.

Trunks and branches are made of wood, which is very strong. Their job is to hold the tree upright and make sure its leaves are facing the sunshine.

The wind won't blow this tree down because its roots are deep and strong.

Roots act like anchors, holding the tree in place. They also take in water from the soil. Trees need water to live, just like you need it to live too!

Did you know?
Almost half of every tree is underground! Tree roots are not easy to see, but they have very important jobs to do.

5

Let's look at leaves

Leaves use the light from the sun to make food for trees. This process is called photosynthesis.

Sunlight gives the leaves the energy they need to change **carbon dioxide** and water into food.

Oxygen is a gas that is released through the process of **photosynthesis**. This is good for humans because we need **oxygen** to breathe.

Carbon dioxide is a gas in the air that gets inside the leaf through tiny holes in the leaf surface.

Sugar is also made during photosynthesis and is food for trees. It moves to all the other parts of the tree.

Water travels all the way from the roots to the leaf. Most of the water leaves the leaf through **evaporation**.

Hooray for trees!

What Happens?

Photosynthesis is possible because of something inside the leaf called **chlorophyll**. Chlorophyll uses energy from sunlight to help the leaf mix the water and carbon dioxide together to make sugar.

All shapes and sizes

Leaves come in different shapes and sizes, but they are usually green. This is because leaves contain chlorophyll, which is green in color.

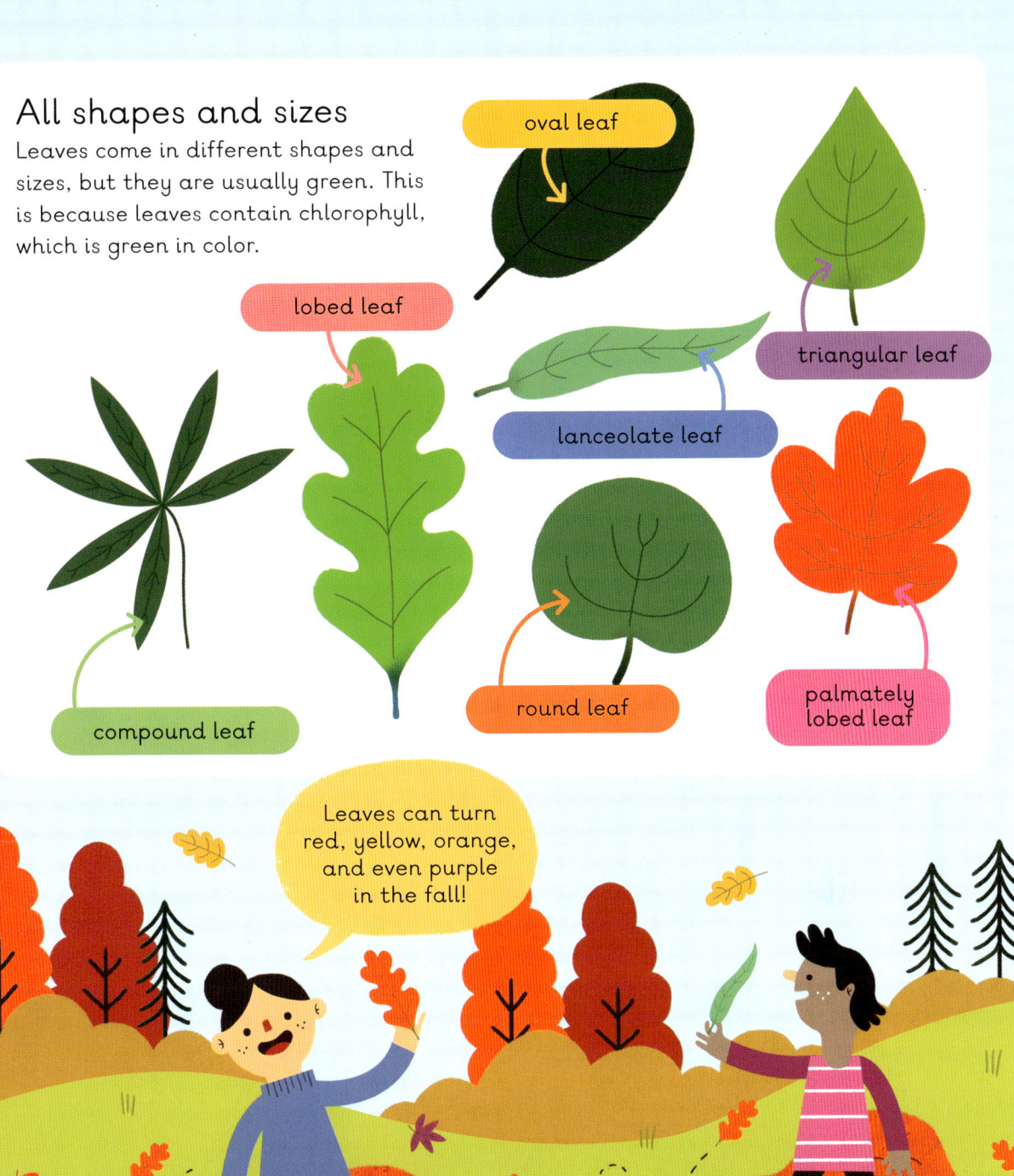

oval leaf

triangular leaf

lobed leaf

lanceolate leaf

compound leaf

round leaf

palmately lobed leaf

Leaves can turn red, yellow, orange, and even purple in the fall!

Did you know?

Trees drop their leaves when it's cold, but before they do they use up all of their chlorophyll. When the green chlorophyll is gone, the autumn leaves turn many different colors.

Start a leaf collection

Collect and keep leaves in a scrapbook. How many types of leaves can you find?

Tool kit

- roll of paper towels
- two pieces of letter-size cardboard
- collected leaves
- two heavy books
- sticky tape
- scrapbook

What to do

1 Layer four sheets of paper towel on top of one of the pieces of cardboard.

2 Place some leaves on top of the paper towels. Make sure the leaves are flat and spread out so they are not touching each other.

You can press more than one layer of leaves, but you will need to use more paper towels and add more books on top.

Did you know?

Leaves are mostly made of water! If you want to keep them for a long time, you need to make sure that they are completely dry.

3 Layer four more sheets of paper towel on top of the leaves. Put another piece of cardboard on top of the paper towels.

4 Put two heavy books on top of the cardboard.

5 Store it in a warm place for about three weeks.

6 When the leaves are dry, take them out gently and carefully tape them into your scrapbook.

Try this...

Collect different leaves during each season and organize your scrapbook into four sections with one for spring, summer, fall, and winter.
Your collection will show how leaves change during the year.

Fallen leaves

Can you match each tree
to its fallen leaf?

In the fall hazel trees make hazelnuts, which are very tasty.

The bark of willow trees has been used for healing and pain relief for centuries around the world.

Maple syrup is made from the sugar maple tree, which grows in North America. The maple leaf is on the Canadian flag.

Holly is an **evergreen** tree with prickly leaves that do not fall off the tree in the winter.

The wood from oak trees was used to make big wooden ships for sailing far out to sea.

Many birch trees have white bark that peels off like paper and can be used to make canoes!

From seed to tree

Without animals or wind, trees wouldn't be able to make seeds and no new trees would grow.

Making seeds

To make seeds, the flowers on a tree need **pollen**. The pollen must be carried from one part of a flower to another part of a different flower. This is called **pollination**.

Insects like big, colorful flowers the most.

Sometimes insects carry pollen from one flower to another.

These flowers don't need to attract insects, so they aren't colorful.

Sometimes the wind can blow the pollen through the air to another flower.

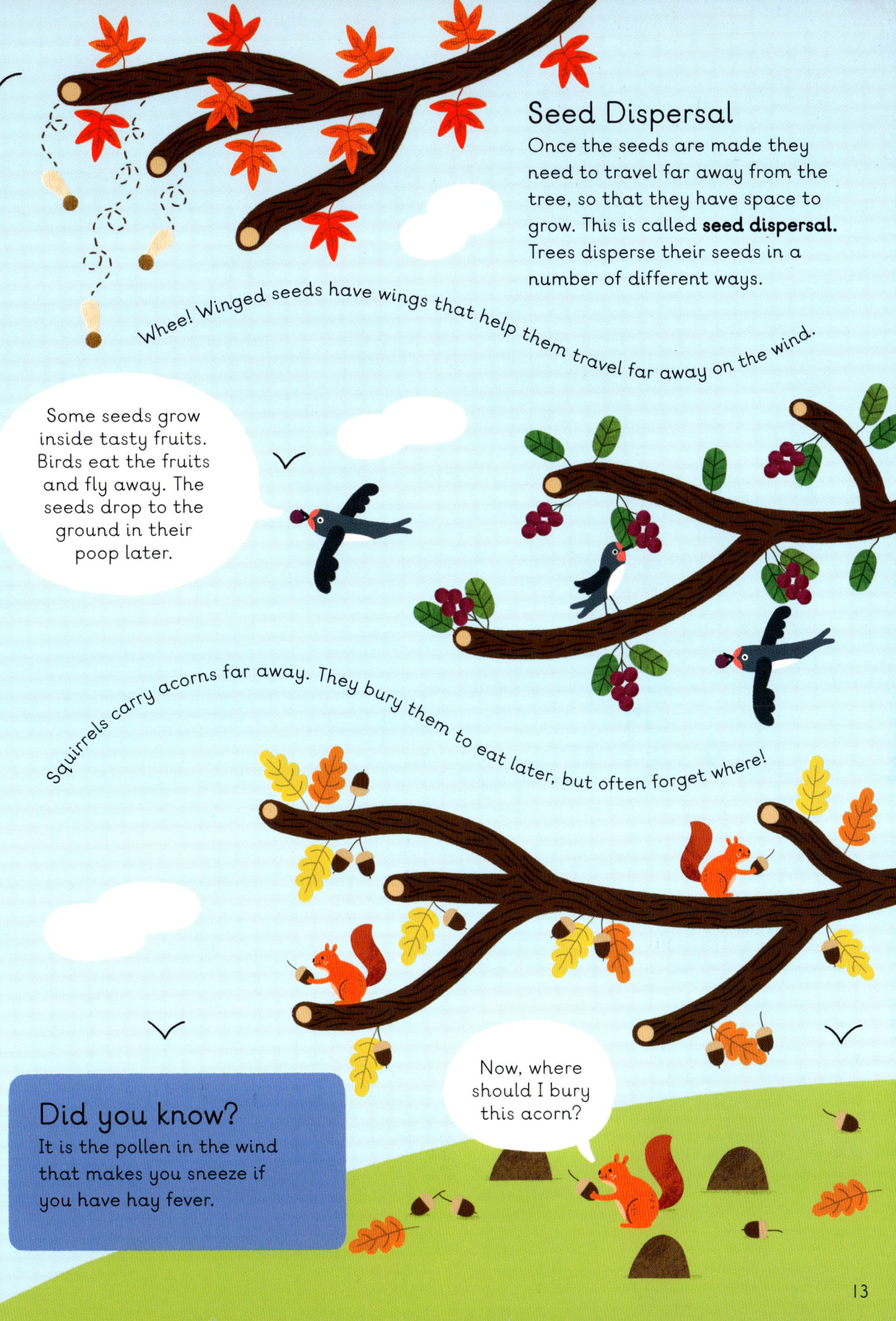

Seed Dispersal

Once the seeds are made they need to travel far away from the tree, so that they have space to grow. This is called **seed dispersal**. Trees disperse their seeds in a number of different ways.

Whee! Winged seeds have wings that help them travel far away on the wind.

Some seeds grow inside tasty fruits. Birds eat the fruits and fly away. The seeds drop to the ground in their poop later.

Squirrels carry acorns far away. They bury them to eat later, but often forget where!

Now, where should I bury this acorn?

Did you know?
It is the pollen in the wind that makes you sneeze if you have hay fever.

13

How far from home?

How far do you think different types of seeds will travel? Test them in this scientific experiment.

What to do

Which seed type will travel the farthest when it drops from a tree?

I predict this seed will travel the farthest because it has wings.

Seed number	Winged/ Not winged	Distance traveled
1	NW	1 ft
2	W	3 ft
3	NW	
4	NW	
5	NW	
6	W	
7	W	
8	W	

1 Look at your seeds and make a **prediction**. Which seed do you think will travel the farthest and why?

2 Fill out the boxes on your record table with what you know and write your prediction at the top.

3 Ask your adult to help you find a safe high place to drop your seeds from. Drop a seed and ask someone to mark where it lands.

4 Measure the distance along the ground from where you dropped the seed to where it landed. Write this number on your record table.

5 Compare the **data** for all your seeds. Which seed type traveled the farthest?

The seed with the highest number traveled the farthest.

That winged seed traveled 25 ft. I'll write that down.

Was your prediction correct?

What happens?
Winged seeds spin around, keeping them in the air longer. This makes it more likely that a gust of wind will catch them, so they can travel further away from the tree.

A hedge for your window

Plant your very own hedge to decorate your window. Care for it and watch it grow.

Tool kit

- egg carton
- scissors
- gloves
- soil (or potting soil)
- spray bottle
- collected tree seeds

What to do

1 Cut the lid off the egg carton.

Wear gloves when handling any soil.

2 Put soil in each egg hole so that they are almost full, then spray with water.

3 Place five seeds in each egg hole. Cover with more soil and spray with more water.

4 Store your egg carton in a warm place for a few weeks. Spray water on the soil in the morning and evening.

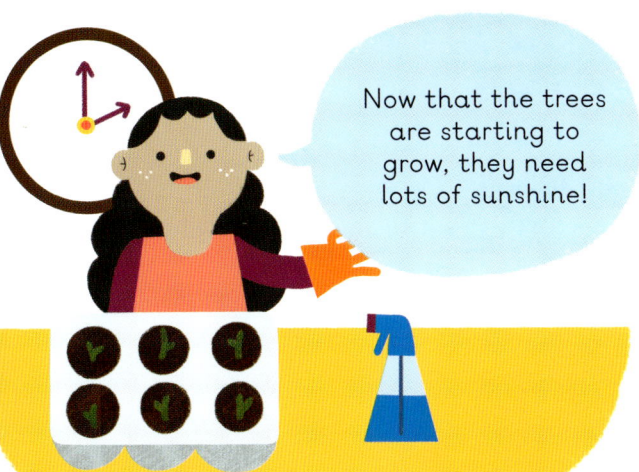

Now that the trees are starting to grow, they need lots of sunshine!

Did you know?

Seeds need warmth and water to start growing, but they don't need any light until they start to poke out of the soil.

5 When the trees start poking through the soil, move them to the windowsill so they have light to grow.

Make sure you keep the soil moist so the trees always have water to drink.

Try this...

Watch your hedge get taller and thicker. After it has been growing for a few weeks, you can trim the leaves with scissors to give the hedge a shape you like. But only cut off small pieces at a time.

Needles and scales

Many trees have wide, flat leaves. They are called **broadleaf** trees. There is another group of trees called **conifers**, which look very different!

Needles

The leaves of many conifers are called **needles** because that is what they look like. They are long and thin, and they often have pointy tips.

Larch

Pine

Spruce

I can see why they are called needles. This spruce branch is prickly!

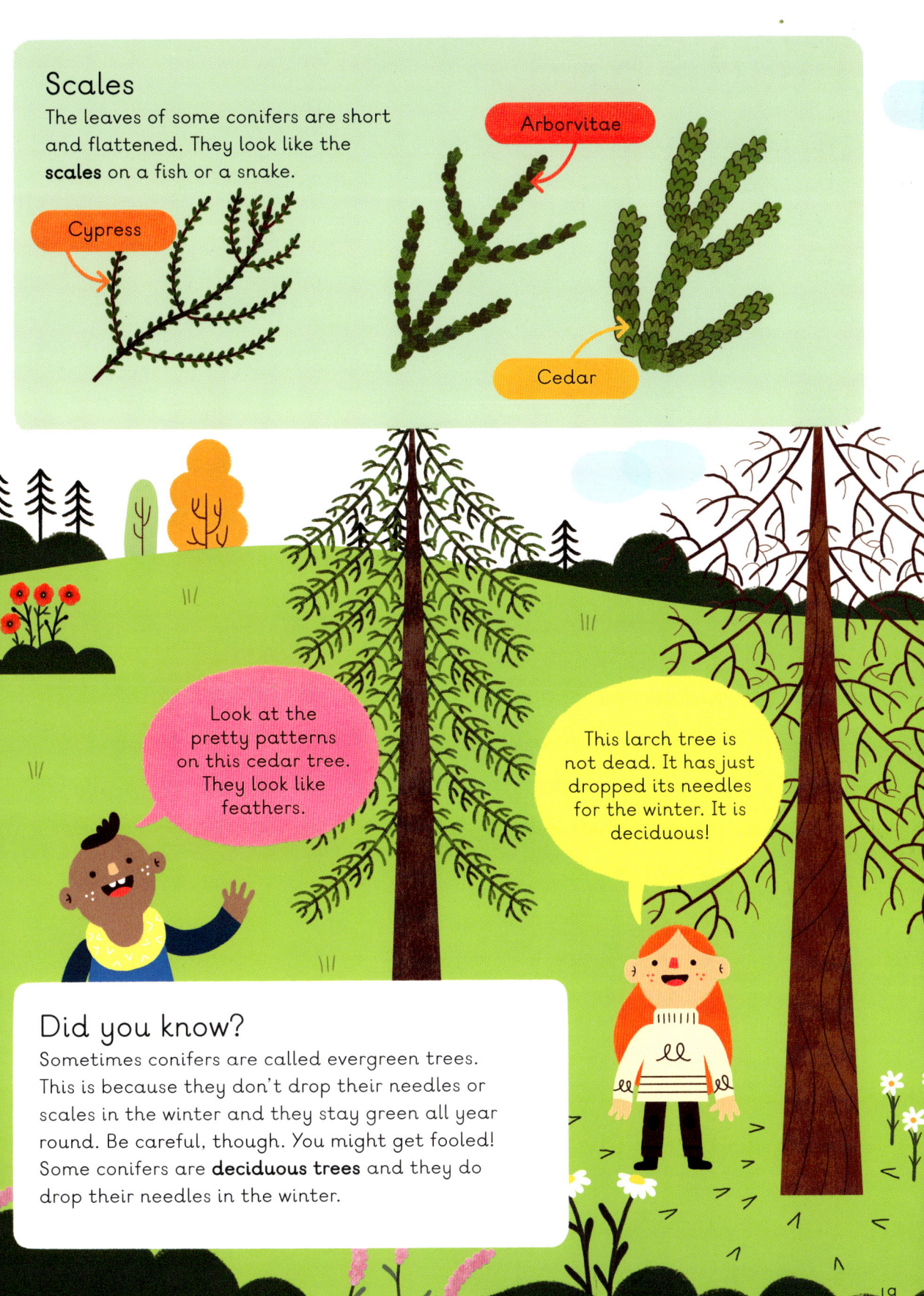

Scales

The leaves of some conifers are short and flattened. They look like the **scales** on a fish or a snake.

Cypress

Arborvitae

Cedar

Look at the pretty patterns on this cedar tree. They look like feathers.

This larch tree is not dead. It has just dropped its needles for the winter. It is deciduous!

Did you know?

Sometimes conifers are called evergreen trees. This is because they don't drop their needles or scales in the winter and they stay green all year round. Be careful, though. You might get fooled! Some conifers are **deciduous trees** and they do drop their needles in the winter.

Inside and outside

Let's take a close look at the trunk of a tree.

Trees can grow big and tall because their trunks and branches are made of wood.

Wood

Wood is made up of **cells**. Each wood cell is long and hollow. They are very small but there are millions of them in a tree. These cells are all held tightly together with a very sticky glue-like substance. This means that wood is very strong!

Did you know?

Because wood cells are hollow, wood is like millions of tiny straws all glued together. This is very useful for the tree. Water from the roots moves through these hollow cells, all the way up to the leaves.

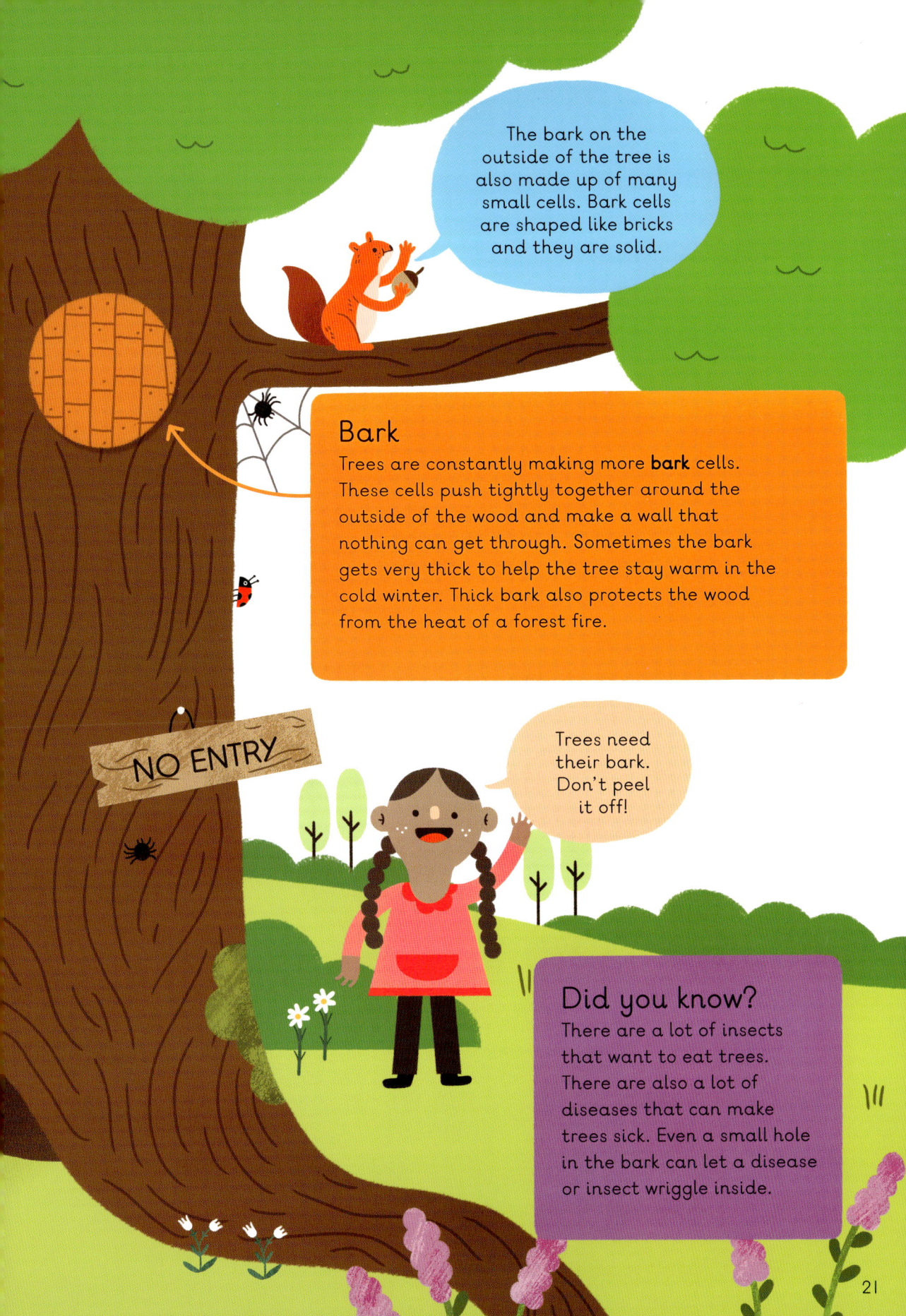

The bark on the outside of the tree is also made up of many small cells. Bark cells are shaped like bricks and they are solid.

Bark

Trees are constantly making more **bark** cells. These cells push tightly together around the outside of the wood and make a wall that nothing can get through. Sometimes the bark gets very thick to help the tree stay warm in the cold winter. Thick bark also protects the wood from the heat of a forest fire.

NO ENTRY

Trees need their bark. Don't peel it off!

Did you know?

There are a lot of insects that want to eat trees. There are also a lot of diseases that can make trees sick. Even a small hole in the bark can let a disease or insect wriggle inside.

Tree bark art

Discover the many different types of tree bark by using them for drawings.

Tool kit
- letter-size paper
- paint roller and tray (or a rolling pin with a towel wrapped around it)
- acrylic or poster paint
- colored pencils

What to do

This tree has long, wiggly grooves in its bark that look like waves.

Try not to tear the paper while you are rolling.

1 Hold a piece of paper against a tree with one hand. See if you can find trees with different types of bark.

2 Cover the roller with paint and gently roll it up and down over the paper. You will get an imprint of the bark on the paper.

3 Take the paper down from the tree and find a flat place to do your drawing.

4 Draw around the shapes made by the bark imprints on the paper. Add color with the colored pencils.

Make some cone decorations

Use some color and your imagination to turn conifer cones into decorations for your home.

Tool kit

- collected cones
- paint and paintbrush
- glue
- glitter
- ribbon

What to do

1 Collect lots of different cones. Look on the ground under trees but also on branches.

2 Place the cones in a warm place to dry for about a week.

3 Use paint, glitter, and your imagination to decorate the cones.

4 Tie a ribbon around the base of each cone. Hang them up to decorate your home.

Did you know?

Conifer trees don't make fruit to hold their seeds like an apple tree does. Instead, conifers protect their seeds in cones. These cones have lots of overlapping scales that are stiff and usually brown in color. There are many different shapes and sizes of cones and they make good decorations.

Pine

Cypress

Larch

I made a table decoration with my pinecones.

Try this...

Try different ways of coloring your cones: paint them all the same color or paint each scale a different color. You could even spread some glue on the cones and sprinkle glitter on them to make the cones sparkle.

Ancient wonders

The oldest person in the world lived to the age of 122 years! Can you guess the age of the oldest tree in the world?

Name: Giant Sequoia
Home: United States
Age: about 3,200 years

Name: Kauri
Home: New Zealand
Age: about 2,000 years

Name: Olive
Home: Greece
Age: about 3,500 years

For some trees, 122 years would be old. But for many trees, this is a very young age indeed!

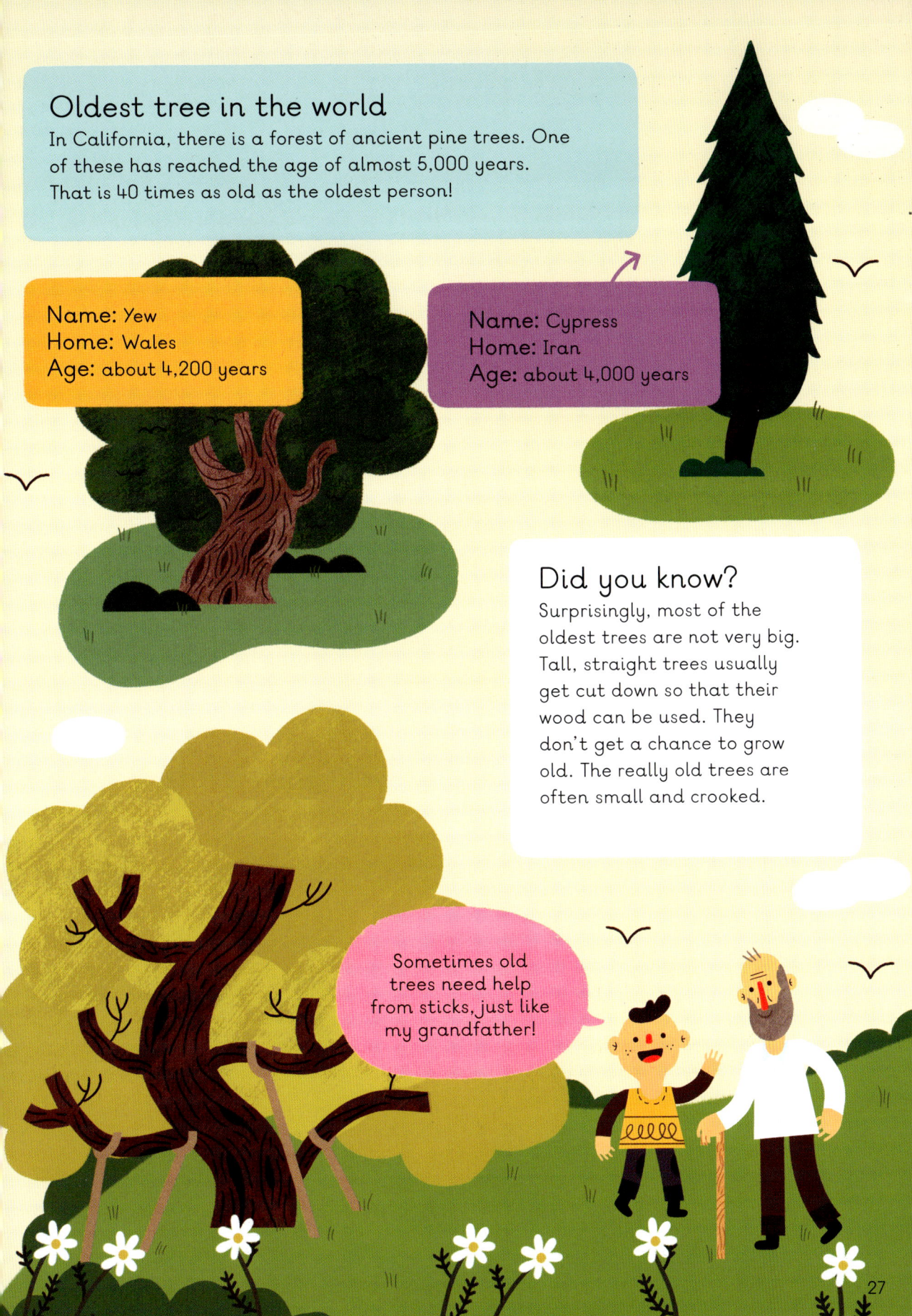

Oldest tree in the world

In California, there is a forest of ancient pine trees. One of these has reached the age of almost 5,000 years. That is 40 times as old as the oldest person!

Name: Yew
Home: Wales
Age: about 4,200 years

Name: Cypress
Home: Iran
Age: about 4,000 years

Did you know?

Surprisingly, most of the oldest trees are not very big. Tall, straight trees usually get cut down so that their wood can be used. They don't get a chance to grow old. The really old trees are often small and crooked.

Sometimes old trees need help from sticks, just like my grandfather!

How old is that tree?

Find out how old the trees around you are by using these simple tricks.

Tree rings

Trees grow a new layer of wood every year, which creates **tree rings**. The rings can be seen on a tree stump or a cut branch, and you can count them to work out how old the tree is.

Tool kit

- magnifying glass
- different color push pins
- measuring tape
- record table

What to do

1 Method one: find a tree that has been cut down, or a branch that has been cut off a tree.

2 Look closely with the magnifying glass and count the rings, starting from the outside.

3 Put some push pins in the tree rings at special years for you.

Tree hugs

Trees grow about ¾ in (2 cm) in **circumference** every year. So you can estimate the age of a tree without having to cut it down by measuring around the tree.

4. Method two: measure the distance around the tree in cm with the measuring tape.

5. Write the measurement in your record table as the circumference for Tree 1.

6. Divide the circumference by two. Write this number in the record table for the age of Tree 1.

The circumference of this tree is 200 cm.

Wow! That means the tree is about 100 years old.

Try this...

Work with your friends to measure 10 trees and fill up your record table. For big trees, you will need to get a friend to help you by holding one end of the measuring tape while you walk around the tree with the other end.

How tall is that tree?

It is easy to measure how tall you are, but how do you measure a tree when the top is so high up?

Tool kit

- a stick
- measuring tape

What to do

1 Find a stick that is the same length as the distance between your chin and the end of your fingers.

2 Hold the bottom of the stick, keeping your arm and the stick straight. This makes a triangle shape with two sides of equal length.

3 Walk backward from the tree you are measuring. Stop every few steps to look and compare the length of the stick you're holding with the tree.

4 Keep moving back until the tree looks the same size as the stick. Stop and put the stick on the ground by your feet.

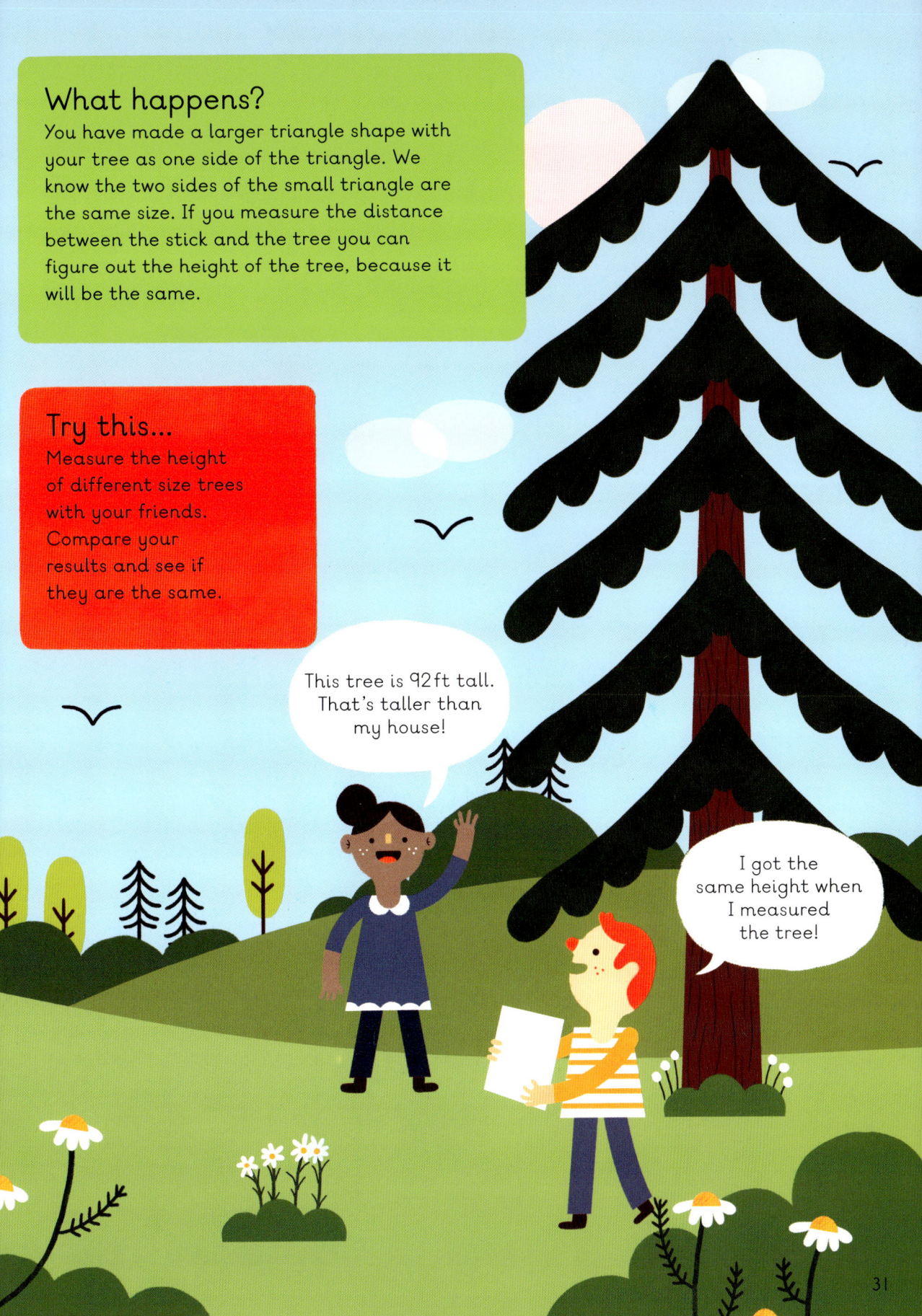

What happens?
You have made a larger triangle shape with your tree as one side of the triangle. We know the two sides of the small triangle are the same size. If you measure the distance between the stick and the tree you can figure out the height of the tree, because it will be the same.

Try this...
Measure the height of different size trees with your friends. Compare your results and see if they are the same.

This tree is 92ft tall. That's taller than my house!

I got the same height when I measured the tree!

Touching the stars

Trees are some of the biggest living things on the planet. Just look at how big some of them can be!

The tallest tree in the world is a **coast redwood**, 380 ft (115 m), in California. It is about as tall as 36 school buses stacked on top of each other.

The **Australian mountain ash**, 327 ft (100 m), is the tallest tree in Australia. It is as tall as a soccer field is long!

The Statue of Liberty in New York City is 305 ft (93 m) tall.

Try this...

Find the height of the trees by using the ruler. Compare the heights of the trees with the heights of the famous buildings mentioned on this page.

130 m

120 m

110 m

100 m

90 m

80 m

70 m

Welcome guests

Over time, trees become homes for lots of animals and other plants.

Birds build their nests in high branches.

Ivy grows around tree trunks.

Deer like the shelter and protection that trees give.

Mosses often grow on the tree bark.

It is safe and warm here, and there is plenty for me to eat.

Did you know?

In the northern **hemisphere**, moss usually grows on the north side of tree trunks. So a tree is like a compass with the moss pointing north.

Squirrels stay in branches for safety, and to find nuts and seeds to eat.

If we take care of this one tree, we are also taking care of all these other plants and animals as well!

Some birds, like woodpeckers, dig holes in the tree trunk. They make holes to find insects to eat and they make holes to build their nests in.

Many different types of insects and spiders live on trees. They are looking for food and for places to hide.

Mushrooms grow at the foot of trees. Earthworms and insects live on the ground, or underground among the roots.

Happy homes

Trees make happy and safe homes for many living things. They provide food to eat, shelter from the weather, and places to hide from danger. This makes trees a good **habitat** for both plants and animals. A single tree can be home to hundreds of types of plants and animals!

Make a tree hotel

Use different parts of trees to attract animal visitors to your backyard.

Tool kit

- gloves
- tree leaves, twigs, branches, and logs
- large pieces of cardboard
- clear tape

What to do

Wear gloves when collecting leaves and wood.

1 The hotel will have four rooms. Collect leaves and pile them near the edge of your backyard to make the Leaf Room.

2 Collect small twigs and place them in a pile next to the leaves to make the Twig Room.

3 Find larger sticks or branches on the ground. Don't break branches from trees. Make a pile of these to make the Branch Room.

4 Find some small logs. Make a pile of these to make the Log Room.

You can use pieces of firewood if you can't find logs.

Try this...

Give your hotel a name. Make a sign out of cardboard and write your hotel name on it. Tape the sign to a twig and stick it in the ground near your hotel. You could make signs with names for each room as well.

LEAF ROOM

THE OAK INN

Watch closely

Keep watch over your hotel to see who is visiting. The best times to see visitors are when you get up in the morning and just before you go to bed at night.

TWIG ROOM

BRANCH ROOM

LOG ROOM

What happens?

The different piles of tree materials which make up your hotel create new habitats. These provide shelter and food to many different animals. So your hotel will increase the **biodiversity** of your backyard.

Trees around the world

Travel around the world and visit some special trees.

The sugar maple tree grows in Canada and New England. The broadleaf forests here are some of the most colorful in the world in the fall.

It rains a lot on the Pacific coast of North America, making it the best habitat for the world's tallest trees.

The Amazon rain forest in South America has the highest biodiversity of any forest in the world. Many different trees grow here.

The monkey puzzle tree grows in central Chile. It has sharp, triangular leaves and even monkeys can't climb it.

N

The Major Oak in Sherwood Forest, **England**, is believed to have been home to Robin Hood and his merry men many years ago.

The Crooked Forest in **Poland** is a group of pine trees that are all curved at the base. No one knows why they are this shape.

The Chapel Oak in **France** is hollow in the middle and has a church built inside it. It has an upstairs and downstairs, and people attend services on Sundays.

The boreal forest is the largest forest in the world. It is made up of conifers and it covers most of **Russia**, northern **Canada**, and northern **Europe**.

The Lost Tree is an acacia tree. It stands alone in the Sahara Desert in **Africa**.

The baobab tree is a common tree in **Madagascar**.

The Gloucester Tree is a karri tree in **Australia**. It has a ladder built into its trunk and, if you are brave, you can climb up 190ft (60m), to the top.

Trees and global warming

The temperature of the air around Earth is rising, and this is causing lots of problems. Trees can come to the rescue and help stop this.

Global warming
Cars and factories release gases and other harmful substances when they burn fuel.

The gases are called **greenhouse gases**. They sit in the **atmosphere**, acting like the glass of a greenhouse.

The sun's rays can easily pass through the greenhouse gases and warm Earth.

Carbon dioxide is a greenhouse gas.

But the heat from the Earth cannot escape back up through the gases, just like heat cannot escape through the glass in a greenhouse. It is trapped, and this makes the temperature rise.

Trees to the rescue

Trees can help get rid of the greenhouse gases in the air. Carbon dioxide is a greenhouse gas and trees use carbon dioxide for photosynthesis. By planting more trees, we can help slow down **global warming** and keep our planet happy.

Remember: trees take in carbon dioxide and release oxygen, which is good for us and the planet!

The heat from Earth can now escape back into space. The temperature does not rise.

When there are lots of trees growing there will be fewer greenhouse gases.

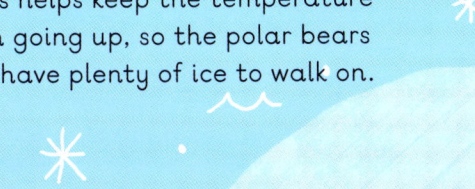

Did you know?

Planting trees can help polar bears! Global warming is melting a lot of ice on the ocean near the North Pole. This means that polar bears can't get to their food. Planting trees helps keep the temperature from going up, so the polar bears still have plenty of ice to walk on.

What do trees give us?

Look around you. How many of the things that you see every day come from trees?

Food
We get a lot of yummy things to eat from trees, including fruits and nuts, and maple syrup for pancakes. Yum!

Wood
The wood in the trunk and branches is cut up and used to make many useful things, such as houses, ships, furniture, and firewood.

Paper
Books, newspapers, and the paper you write on are made from the wood of trees.

Arts and crafts

Trees inspire creativity! We can use cones for painting, leaves for rubbings, and branches for wreaths.

Trees also give us things to play with, like strong branches for a tree house...

...a swing,

...or even just shade on a hot day.

Did you know?

There are people called foresters who manage our forests. When we cut down trees for important wood products, foresters plant new trees to replace them.

Make your own paper

Use recyclable materials to make your own colorful paper.

What to do

Use old newspapers, writing paper, or even cardboard egg cartons. Don't use anything shiny or waxy.

1 Tear the recyclable materials into small pieces. Put them into the blender with water and leave to soak for 20 minutes.

2 Ask an adult to help you blend the mixture into a smooth pulp.

3 Place a sheet of waxed paper on a dish towel and then scoop the pulp onto it.

Try this...

You can make your paper more fun by stirring in food coloring or flower petals after the pulp is made.

4 Place another sheet of waxed paper on top of the pulp. Use a rolling pin to flatten the pulp into a thin layer.

5 Carefully peel the waxed paper off. Your pulp is now a sheet of new paper.

6 Lay a dry dish towel on top of the wet sheet of new paper. Gently roll over the dish towel to soak up water from the sheet.

It might take a few days to dry completely.

The paper is now ready for writing or drawing.

7 Carefully peel the dish towel off. Place your new paper in a warm place to dry.

8 Carefully peel your new sheet of paper from the waxed paper. Use the scissors to trim it to the size and shape you want.

Glossary

Atmosphere The mixture of gases which make up the air around Earth.

Bark The thick, protective outer layer of a tree.

Biodiversity The number of different types of plants and animals that live in an area.

Broadleaf tree A type of tree with wide, flat leaves.

Carbon dioxide A gas in the air around Earth that trees use to make their food. It also causes global warming.

Chlorophyll A chemical in leaves that takes in energy from the sun to make food. Chlorophyll gives leaves their green color.

Cells All living things are made up of cells. Cells are very small and they come in many shapes. They pack together to make the bodies of plants and animals.

Circumference The distance measured around the outside of a circular shape.

Conifer A tree whose leaves look like needles or scales and usually stay on the tree all year round.

Data Numbers that you get from measuring something in an experiment

Deciduous tree A tree that loses its leaves in the winter.

Evaporation The process of liquid turning into a gas.

Evergreen tree A tree that holds on to its leaves all year long and does not lose them in the winter.

Global warming The slow rise in Earth's average temperature.

Greenhouse gas A gas in the air around Earth that causes global warming. Greenhouse gases let sunshine through but keep the heat from escaping back into space.

Habitat The home of a plant or animal, where it can find shelter and food.

Hemisphere Half of a round shape. Earth can be divided into a northern and southern hemisphere, or into an eastern and western hemisphere.

Needle A type of leaf that looks like a needle and is found on coniferous trees.

Oxygen A gas in the air around Earth that we need to breathe. Trees produce oxygen when they make their food.

Photosynthesis This is how leaves use the sun's energy to make food. Sugar is made by combining water and carbon dioxide gas.

Pollen A yellow powder made by male flowers. It is made up of millions of tiny particles called pollen grains.

Pollination When pollen is moved from one part of a flower to another part of a flower to make a new seed.

Prediction A guess about what will happen in the future.

Scales Small flat leaves that look like scales and grow on coniferous trees.

Seed dispersal The movement of new seeds away from the plant where they were made so that the new plants have enough space to grow.

Tree rings The rings on the inside of a tree that are created by growth.

Brimming with creative inspiration, how-to projects, and useful information to enrich your everyday life, Quarto Knows is a favorite destination for those pursuing their interests and passions. Visit our site and dig deeper with our books into your area of interest: Quarto Creates, Quarto Cooks, Quarto Homes, Quarto Lives, Quarto Drives, Quarto Explores, Quarto Gifts, or Quarto Kids.

This edition published in 2021 by Chartwell Books,
an imprint of The Quarto Group
142 West 36th Street, 4th Floor
New York, NY 10018 USA
T (212) 779-4972 F (212) 779-6058
www.QuartoKnows.com

First published in 2018 by QEB Publishing,
an imprint of The Quarto Group,
6 Orchard Road, Suite 100
Lake Forest, CA 92630

10 9 8 7 6 5 4 3 2 1

Chartwell titles are also available at discount for retail, wholesale, promotional, and bulk purchase. For details, contact the Special Sales Manager by email at specialsales@quarto.com or by mail at The Quarto Group, Attn: Special Sales Manager, 100 Cummings Center Suite 265D, Beverly, MA 01915, USA.

ISBN: 978-0-7858-3971-2

Author: Kevin Warwick
Illustrator: Pau Morgan
Consultant: Fred Hageneder
Editor: Ellie Brough
Designer: Clare Barber

Printed in China

Not for individual sale.